COLLEGE OF ALAMEDA LIBRARY

✓

W

D0872314

JF
1001   Farquharson, Robin
F33   Theory of voting.

DATE DUE

JUN 22 30			
DEC 6 '7			
NOV 21 '8			
MAR 9 '88			
DEC 2 92			

LENDING POLICY
IF YOU DAMAGE OR LOSE LIBRARY
MATERIALS, THEN YOU WILL BE
CHARGED FOR REPLACEMENT. FAIL
URE TO PAY AFFECTS LIBRARY
PRIVILEGES, GRADES, TRANSCRIPTS,
DIPLOMAS AND REGISTRATION
PRIVILEGES OR ANY COMBINATION
THEREOF

THEORY OF VOTING

Recipient of the 1961 Monograph Prize of the
American Academy of Arts and Sciences in the
field of the social sciences

THEORY OF VOTING

by
Robin Farquharson

New Haven, Yale University Press
1969

Copyright © 1969 by Yale University.

All rights reserved. This book may not be
reproduced, in whole or in part, in any form
(except by reviewers for the public press),
without written permission from the publishers.

Library of Congress catalog card number: 70-81417

Standard book number: 300-01121-0

Designed by John O. C. McCrillis,
set in Baskerville type,
and printed in the United States of America by
the Carl Purington Rollins Printing-Office of
the Yale University Press, New Haven, Connecticut.
Distributed in Continental Europe
by Yale University Press Ltd., London; in
Canada by McGill-Queen's University Press, Montreal; and
in Mexico by Centro Interamericano de Libros
Académicos, Mexico City.

TO ROBERT SHACKLETON

Contents

Foreword by Martin Shubik

It is an honor and a pleasure to write the foreword to this book, which is a highly original and important contribution to the theory of voting. A completely new and natural way of looking at all voting procedures in terms of a noncooperative game is presented.

By using a beautifully lucid game theory approach to all binary voting procedures, Dr. Farquharson shows how the Condorcet paradox is related to the strategic aspects of sequential voting. Concepts such as sincere, straightforward, or sophisticated voting are introduced, and each one adds considerably to our understanding of the strategic structure underlying every voting process.

Farquharson is concerned with the same problems dealt with by Kenneth Arrow in *Social Choice and Individual Values*, but Arrow limits his analysis of voting and preferences to nonstrategic, independent, direct optimizing behavior by individuals. This limitation is in the same spirit as the behavioral assumptions made in the general equilibrium models of the price system.

Some game theoretic or competitive analyses of the political voting process have been made recently. They fall into two major categories, both of which are completely different from this work. The first has been devoted to the construction of a "power" index to measure the importance of an individual as a function of the distribution of votes. Articles by Harsanyi, Mann, Riker, Shapley, Shubik, and others deal with this. The second deals with parties and aggregates of individuals rather

than with the rational voter either as an individual isolated maximizer or as a player. The works of Buchanan,
Downs, Kramer, Riker, Shubik, Tullock, Wilson, and
others provide examples.

As with every important book, more questions are
posed than answered. In particular, in an appendix a
sketch is given of a theory involving group stability in
voting where the equilibrium is immune to defections
by groups. Farquharson uses only the ordinal properties
of individual preferences. It would be fascinating to
see how much more can be obtained starting with such
Spartan fare.

Farquharson has opened up much new terrain for ex-
ploration. Can we characterize classes of voting systems
according to the amount of sophisticated voting to be
encountered, i.e., by the amount to which people do not
vote directly in accord with their preferences? What are
the limiting characteristics of large voting games of this
variety when the number of individuals and/or the number of issues become large? Can we extend his analysis to
include games with unknown preferences, where, for
example, a government is drawing up a constitution that
will specify the voting process, but it has only probability
estimates on the preference scales of the citizens?

This is a very non-esoteric book. Together with its logical
elegance and use of game theory it conveys a deep con-
cern with and understanding of voting procedures as they
are. The examples are a delight. It is a great shame that
publication has been delayed for over a decade. In spite
of this unfortunate delay the power and novelty of the
ideas have been by no means diminished by the passage
of time.

Preface

In 1953, while studying international relations at Oxford, I was struck by the result of the voting in the United States Senate on the League of Nations Covenant after the First World War. It seemed that the tactics of those concerned had produced a result desired by few, and I asked myself whether this was because of the two-thirds majority rule. I began to play with numerical examples, and soon rediscovered Condorcet's voting paradox in which voters with consistent individual preferences show inconsistent collective preferences, even without a two-thirds majority requirement. My then tutor, Mr. Norman Leyland, directed my attention to the works of Kenneth Arrow and Duncan Black. I found, however, that they both assumed that voters used neither strategy nor skill, while Von Neumann and Morgenstern, to whom their footnotes referred me, had not applied the theory of games to actual voting procedures.

I set out to fill the gap, and during 1953-55 constructed game-theoretical representations of many varieties of actual voting procedures. The definition of "determinacy" which I worked out for such procedures proved to be the same as one which had, unknown to me, already been applied by David Gale to quite different games. I succeeded in obtaining solutions of this type for all "binary" voting procedures and a wide class of other procedures. The two theorems of the monograph apply to binary procedures with an unlimited number of voters and outcomes. The particular results of Appendix I have been set out only for the case of three voters and three outcomes, but can readily be extended to cover any desired number of either. In their present form they can be considered as providing the logical basis for a theory of "troikas" in the sense of N. Khrushchev.

This monograph was begun while I was an undergraduate at Brasenose College, Oxford, and completed during a Research Studentship at Nuffield College, and a Laming Travelling Fellowship at The Queen's College. In 1958 it was accepted for the degree of Doctor of Philosophy in the University of Oxford, under the title "An Approach to a Pure Theory of Voting Procedure".

My special thanks are due my university supervisor, Mr. D. N. Chester, Warden of Nuffield College, and my college supervisor, Professor D. G. Champernowne. I am particularly grateful also to Professor Kenneth Arrow, Mr. Jonathan Bennett, Professor R. B. Braithwaite, Mr. Michael Dummett, Mr. Denis A. Higgs, Dr. Colin Leys, Dr. Ian Little, Dr. John R. Searle, and Dr. Martin Shubik.

R.F.

When actual objects are counted, or when geometry or dynamics are applied to actual space or actual matter, or when, in any other way, mathematical reasoning is applied to what exists, the reasoning employed has a form not dependent upon the objects to which it is applied being just those objects that they are, but only upon their having certain general properties.

In pure mathematics, actual objects in the world of existence will never be in question, but only hypothetical objects having those general properties upon which depends whatever deduction is being considered: and these general properties will always be expressible in terms of the fundamental concepts which I have called logical constants.

Thus when space or motion is spoken of in pure mathematics, it is not actual space or actual motion, as we know them in experience, that are spoken of, but any entity possessing those abstract general properties of space or motion that are employed in the reasonings of geometry or dynamics. The question whether these properties belong, as a matter of fact, to actual space or actual motion, is irrelevant to pure mathematics, and therefore to the present work, being, in my opinion, a purely empirical question, to be investigated in the laboratory or the observatory.

BERTRAND RUSSELL
The Principles of Mathematics

Introduction

To construct a model is to adopt an idealisation. One replaces the subject of one's enquiry, fallibly perceived and imperfectly understood, by an intellectual substitute: a formal structure whose properties are explicitly assumed, or formally deducible from explicit assumptions. Conclusions about this abstract structure are accessible to the unaided reason, and testable logically within a deductive framework.

This idealisation permits the application of mathematical techniques to the perceptual world. Observation is reduced to order within a system built up from purely formal elements.

For such a system to be of use, it must do two things. First, it must confirm crude experience in elementary cases. Second, it must provide conclusions whose scope extends beyond immediate experience, and which can be put to the test as experience is extended. Experimental falsification of any conclusion indicates that at least one assumption of the model must be modified.

In his Inaugural Lecture, Professor Coulson quoted J. L. Synge:

> The use of applied mathematics in its relation
> to a physical problem involves three steps:
>   i) a dive from the world of reality into the
>   world of mathematics;
> ii) a swim in the world of mathematics;

iii) a climb from the world of mathematics back
into the world of reality, carrying the
prediction in our teeth.[1]

The third step is indispensable.

The theory which will be presented here is intended to
be of use. Though its conclusions are reached by logical
deductions, its assumptions are not logical truths. As an
interpreted theory, it makes synthetic assertions about
particular voting procedures and particular modes of behaviour. Since these assertions are not analytic, they may
be wrong. At least, they are testable. And if they are not
confirmed, it will be certain that (logical slips aside) the
explanation lies in some aspect of the assumptions. Then
the way is clear for these to be reexamined, and a more
fruitful model constructed.

"The goal of political studies is not knowledge, but
action".[2]

1. C. A. Coulson, *The Spirit of Applied Mathematics* (Oxford, Clarendon
Press, 1953), p. 12.
2. Aristotle, *Politics*.

CHAPTER 1.

Voters, Outcomes, and Preferences

The scope of our enquiry may be simply defined: we are concerned with voters who have preferences with respect to outcomes.

These expressions have an ordinary meaning, and we shall seek always to use them so as to preserve that meaning. Nevertheless, they will acquire a status as "terms of art". For we shall need to couch our assumptions in formal language, in order to permit the application of logical techniques. Therefore it will be necessary to put our fundamental terms into correspondence with certain abstract entities, formulated with sufficient precision to be handled within the theory of sets. Thus every term must be understood as a technical term, either taken as primitive or defined by means of primitive terms. The whole structure constitutes a system whose coherence is independent of the ordinary meaning of its expressions, and which may be given diverse interpretations.

In our exposition, however, we shall cling to ordinary meaning and to a single concrete interpretation. We shall set out our primitive terms, and use them to define our further terms, but we shall seek to redeem formality of reasoning by the informality of argument and example.

First, *voters*. We assume that there exist a number of individuals, whose choices have consequences. These voters may compose an electorate, an assembly, or a committee: they may even be viewed as blocs or parties, or nations in conclave. The only essential assumption is that they constitute units, each with the power to choose, and that the choices made by all the individuals determine a result. This result will necessarily be a member of the set of outcomes.

The *outcomes* are the possible results of the process of decision. The voting must eventually terminate with the selection of one or other outcome. The outcomes may be possible courses of action, or various motions and amendments to motions, or various candidates and combinations of candidates. Every possible decision must fall within the set of outcomes; one, and only one, becomes the result.

With regard to the outcomes, each voter has *preferences*. We assume that he could, on demand, express his evaluation of the outcomes by listing them all in order.[1]

This preference scale is assumed to remain constant throughout the course of the voting. It may, of course, have been modified by earlier argument or events, but it does not vary after voting has begun.

These three terms—*voters, outcomes, preferences*[2]—are sufficient to express those aspects of our material to which we shall seek to give precise representation. These three terms have been expounded, but not defined: we shall endeavour to define our subsequent terms wholly by their means.

Let us take an example from the letters of Pliny the Younger.[3] The consul Afranius Dexter had been found slain, and it was uncertain whether he had died by his own hand or at those of his freedmen. When the matter came before the Senate, Pliny wished to acquit them;

---

1. We shall be principally concerned with preference scales on which no two outcomes are ranked equally; such scales we call "strong". A "weak" scale is one on which two or more outcomes are bracketed together as equally desirable.

another senator moved that they should be banished to an island; and a third, that they should be put to death.

There are just three outcomes mentioned:

a) to acquit;
b) to banish;
c) to condemn to death.

We may assume that these possibilities are exhaustive: the set of outcomes thus consists of the set (A,B,C).

We may consider the set of voters as the whole Senate; or, following Pliny, we may suppose there exist three blocs each united in opinion and action, so that there are only three effectively distinct voters.

Each voter's preference scale constitutes a ranking of the members of the set (A,B,C) in order. We shall suppose that there are three effectively distinct scales:

> the *acquitters*, who clearly prefer acquittal to either of the other alternatives. One may presume, further, that they would rather banish than condemn. By

---

2. Formally, we may identify these three with three abstract entities:

a finite set N, composed of n elements, the voters;

a finite set M, composed of m elements, the outcomes;

a family of binary relations R_k, defined in the set M.

We require that, for x,y,z, in M, for $k \in N$

    i) $x\ R_k\ y$ or $y\ R_k\ x$;

    ii) if $x\ R_k\ y$ and $y\ R_k\ z$, then $x\ R_k\ z$.

If $x\ R_k\ y$ and not $y\ R_k\ x$, we write $x\ P_k\ y$, and say "x is preferred to y by k".

If $x\ R_k\ y$ and $y\ R_k\ x$, we write $x\ I_k\ y$, and say "x is indifferent to y by k".

We may read $x\ R_k\ y$ either as "x is not worse than y" or "x is preferred to indifferent to y by k".

Cf. Kenneth Arrow, *Social Choice and Individual Values* (New York, Wiley, 1951); J. R. Hicks, *A Revision of Demand Theory* (Oxford, Clarendon Press, 1956).

3. Book VIII, letter xiv. Reproduced on pages 57-60.

writing "ABC" we shall express their scale in full: A ranked first, B second, and C last.

the *banishers*, who if they cannot banish would rather acquit than condemn to death. Their scale is thus "BAC".

the *condemners*, who if they cannot effect condemnation, would rather banish than acquit. We write this "CBA".

Our "model" of the situation is now a very simple one. We have three outcomes (A,B,C); three voters; and three preference scales, (ABC, BAC, CBA). We shall now proceed to put the model into working order.

CHAPTER 2.

The Structure of Voting Procedures

We have postulated voters and outcomes, with preferences as the link between them. Now we come to consider the process whereby an outcome is selected as the result of the voting.

We shall define a *voting procedure*, initially, in terms of the set of outcomes. Suppose this set divided into two subsets, each subset into two further subsets, and so on until single outcomes are reached.

Such a sequence of divisions may be depicted as a tree, the "outcome tree". Each of its forks corresponds to a division, and the end of each of its branches corresponds to an outcome.[1]

Since each division is into two subsets, we may call such procedures "binary". The class of binary procedures includes those of Parliament, with "Aye" and "No" lobbies, and the usual committee method of voting on amendments to a motion.[2] It also includes some electoral procedures, such as that whereby each candidate is considered in turn for acceptance, and the Scots' practice of election by paired comparisons, in which one candidate is excluded at each division.[3]

---

1. Formally we may postulate a set function f, taking as its values pairs of subsets of M, and as its arguments the set M and *such subsets occurring in its values as contain more than one element.*

2. Sir Walter Citrine, *ABC of Chairmanship* (London, Co-operative Printing Society Ltd., 1939), pp. 60-70.

3. M. Ransom, *The Chairman's and Debater's Handbook* (London, Routledge).

The first procedure which Pliny describes falls within this class. It may be set out in full as follows:

The first division is taken on the issue of acquittal. If acquittal is decided upon, then no further vote is taken.

If acquittal is defeated, then a second division takes place between banishment and condemnation to death.

Thus the first division is between acquittal and conviction; if the freedmen are convicted, the second division decides their punishment.

This procedure corresponds to a first division of the set (A,B,C) into the subsets (A) and (B,C); and a second division of the subset (B,C) into the further subsets (B) and (C).

It may be shown, as in Figure 1, in diagram form[4] as a tree with three endpoints, each representing an outcome.

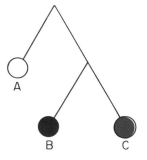

Figure 1
Procedure Ia

In this procedure, outcome A is singled out for first consideration, while outcomes B and C are given identical treatment. We may thus designate it as "Procedure Ia".

4. Here we face a dilemma, since trees grow upward but prose reads downward. We choose to follow the lexicographical convention rather than the botanical.

If the first issue put were that of banishment, we should have Procedure Ib; if condemnation, Procedure Ic.

We may state precisely what form the divisions must take in order to be admissible as composing a procedure. Whenever a set is divided into two subsets, we require

> AXIOM I: Each element of the set is in at least one subset;
>
> AXIOM II: Neither subset is identical with the whole set.[5]

We do *not* require that the two subsets at a division have no members in common. The usual method of procedure on amendments, in fact, includes a division into overlapping subsets. A motion is moved, and an amendment to it proposed. The first division occurs on the issue of whether to amend the motion. If the amendment is adopted, the second division is on the motion as amended; if it is defeated, the second division is on the original motion.

In the senatorial case, this might be conceived as a situation in which a motion is put forward:

> "That the freedmen be condemned to death".

An amendment is moved:

> "That 'condemned to death' be replaced by banished".

The first division would be on whether to amend the motion. If the amendment were defeated, the final division would be between death and acquittal; if the

---

5. Formally, if M is the whole set, and the two subsets are designated as $f_0 (M)$ and $f_1 (M)$, we require:

I: $f_0 (M) \cup f_1 (M) = M$

II: $f_0 (M) \neq M, f_1 (M) \neq M$

amendment were adopted, the final vote would be between acquittal and banishment. Thus acquittal could be reached by two distinct routes.

In this procedure, the set (A,B,C) of outcomes is first divided into (A,B) and (A,C). Each subset is then in turn divided into its component outcomes. The outcome A appears twice among the endpoints: we may designate this procedure therefore as IIa. (See Figure 2)

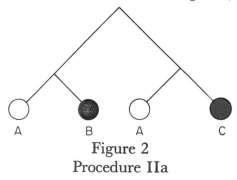

A   B   A   C

Figure 2
Procedure IIa

Similarly we have Procedure IIb in which the first vote is taken between A and C, and the outcome preferred then put against B; and similarly Procedure IIc. These are, however, somewhat less usual.

We have not yet dealt with the means of deciding between the two subsets of outcomes at a division. The two subsets constitute for each voter his available *choices;* he may choose either one or the other.[6] The choices expressed by all the voters determine the subset which is selected.

Such a process may reasonably be called "voting" only if the relation between the individual choices and the collective choice obeys certain conditions.

6. Abstention therefore is excluded.

These conditions amount to requiring that every voter's choice has an effect not unfavourable to the subset chosen, and that each voter is less than a dictator, yet not wholly powerless.

For each voter, we require[7]

AXIOM III: If a choice of a subset does not produce it, choosing the other subset will not either;

AXIOM IV: Any one voter's choice can be outweighed by those of the other voters together;

AXIOM V: Every voter's choice has some weight.

Axioms III-V together entail that there should be at least three voters;[8] they amount in that case to requiring that the vote should be taken by simple majority vote at each division. In the case of more than three voters, they are compatible with a wide variety of procedures, including those in which one voter has a casting vote to break ties, and those in which two-thirds or other special majorities are required.

Clearly, not all procedures are binary. We may first generalise our model to include ternary, quaternary, etc., procedures (or in general, "divisional" procedures). The set of outcomes is divided into a number of subsets, each subset into further subsets, and so on as before until single outcomes are attained.

Our axioms require only slight amendment:

I′ Each element of the set is in at least one subset;

II′ No two subsets are identical;

III′ No subset is identical with the whole set;

IV′ If voting for a subset does not produce it, voting for no other subset will;

V′ Any one voter can be outvoted by the rest together on any issue;

VI′ Every vote has some effect on every issue.

We shall find binary procedures possess many properties lacking in divisional procedures in general, so that assimilation of binary procedures to the general class is inadvisable.

7. Formally, we suppose a decision function g. The result of each division is a function of the voters' choices; like the choices themselves, it takes the values 0 and 1.

If C_k is a choice of the voter k, then $g(C_1, C_2, .. C_k, .. C_n) = 0$ or 1; and an '$(n-1)$-tuple' of the form $(C_1, C_2, .. C_{k-1}, C_{k+1}, .. C_n)$ corresponds to a specification of the choices made by all voters but k. It we denote any instance of such an $(n-1)$-tuple by Y_k, then, for all Y_k, $g(C_k, Y_k) = 0$ or 1.

We restate the axioms:

IV: For every k and every Y_k, $g(0,Y_k) = 1$ entails $g(1,Y_k) = 1$;

V: For every k there is some Y_k such that $g(0,Y_k) = 1$, and some Y_k such that $g(1, Y_k) = 0$;

VI: For every k there is some Y_k such that $g(0,Y_k) \neq g(1,Y_k)$.

Axiom IV corresponds to a special case of Arrow's Condition 2. Axiom V is somewhat stronger than his Condition 5, much weaker than K. O. May's Condition III (*Econometrica*, 1952, pp. 680-84). Axiom VI is related to Arrow's Condition 4, though not by descent.

8. For n = 2 the three axioms are inconsistent.

For n = 3 the axioms are consistent, but not independent: IV and V together imply VI. Examples of functions realising the seven possible truth cases are given below (TTT indicates that all three axioms hold; TTF indicates the case in which axioms IV and V hold, but Axiom VI does not, etc.):

	TTT	TTF	TFT	TFF	FTT	FTF	FFT	FFF
g(0,0,0)	0	—	0	0	0	1	0	1
g(0,0,1)	0	—	0	0	0	0	1	0
g(0,1,0)	0	—	0	0	0	1	0	0
g(0,1,1)	1	—	0	0	1	0	1	0
g(1,0,0)	0	—	0	0	0	0	0	1
g(1,0,1)	1	—	0	0	1	1	1	0
g(1,1,0)	1	—	0	0	1	0	0	0
g(1,1,1)	1	—	1	0	0	1	0	0

The case TTF can only arise if n > 3; for n = 4 it is exemplified by the procedure in which the fourth voter is neglected and the result is determined by the majority choice of the other three. For n = 3 the axioms are categorical; for $n \geq 4$, they are consistent and completely independent.

The simplest ternary procedure for three outcomes is that in which the division into one-element subsets takes place immediately, as in Procedure III, shown in Figure 3.

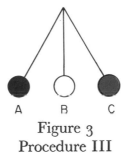

Figure 3
Procedure III

This procedure we may call "simple plurality"—it is the procedure on which Pliny insisted in the example.

Another procedure frequently used is that of "elimination"; the whole set is divided into three two-element subsets, votes taken for each, and then a final vote taken between the two elements of the chosen subset. This procedure has the appearance of Procedure IV, in Figure 4.

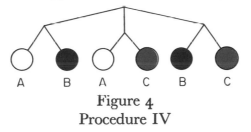

Figure 4
Procedure IV

It is similar to the procedure in which votes are taken *against* each of the three outcomes in the whole set; the set with most such hostile votes is eliminated, and a final vote taken between the other two. (This is also the structure of the game known as "Russian sledge", in which victims are successively thrown to the wolves by vote of a group until only one remains.)

Such procedures are outside this class: a more general framework within which they can be considered will be set out in Chapter 4.

CHAPTER 3.

Sincere Voting

The simplest assumption which can be made about the behaviour of voters is that their votes are directly in accordance with their preference scales.[1] That this assumption was unrealistic was perfectly well known to C. L. Dodgson, who wrote several pamphlets on the subject,[2] and referred to the tendency of voters to adopt a

> principle of voting which makes an election more of a game of skill than a real test of the wishes of the electors, and . . . my own opinion is that it is better for elections to be decided according to the wish of the majority than of those who happen to have most skill at the game.

We shall seek to treat the problem of voting strategy from a game-theoretical viewpoint;[3] nevertheless it is desirable to discuss first of all, as a point of departure, the

---

1. Arrow, *Social Choice and Individual Values*, pp. 7 and 80 n.; and Duncan Black, "On the Rationale of Group Decision-Making", *Journal of Political Economy 56* (1948). See also Duncan Black and R. A. Newing, *Committee Decisions with Complementary Valuation* (London, Hodge, 1951), and its review by L. Goodman, *American Journal of Sociology, 57* (1952), p. 611.

2. *A Method of Taking Votes on More than Two Issues* (unpublished, March 1876, Bodleian Library). Also *A Discussion of the Various Methods of Procedure in Conducting Elections* (Oxford, 1873, Parrish Collection, Princeton University Library), p. 10, and *Suggestions as to the Best Method of Taking Votes* (Oxford, 1874, Bodleian Library).

3. John von Neumann and Oskar Morgenstern, *Theory of Games and Economic Behavior* (3d ed. Princeton, Princeton University Press, 1953).

meaning that can be attached to the idea of "voting directly according to one's preferences".

In the procedure of Figure 1, we may consider a voter of preference-scale ABC—acquittal his first preference, banishment his second, death his last. We say that he is voting *sincerely* if he votes for "A" at the first division, "B" at the second.

In the procedure of Figure 2, he would vote for (A,B) against (A,C): in that of Figure 3, for "A".

We can subsume these examples under a general definition. Call the "top" outcome of a subset that outcome highest on a voter's scale. A voter votes sincerely, then, if he chooses the subset with the highest-ranked top. If the tops are equal, he chooses the subset with the highest-ranked second-to-top element, and so on.[4]

This definition is sufficient to define a unique course of action for each of the classes of procedure we have so far considered.

We have assumed that three groups of voters exist, each less than half of the whole Senate, and each having a distinct scale of preferences.

Under the procedure first mentioned by Pliny, Procedure Ia, the result of sincere voting on the first vote between acquittal and conviction would have been:

For acquittal: acquitters;

For conviction: banishers and condemners.

---

4. A subset x is preferred to a subset y if $\text{Max}(x) P_k \text{Max}(y)$; or when $\text{Max}(x) I_k \text{Max}(y)$, if $\text{Max}(x - \text{Max}(x)) P_k \text{Max}(y - \text{Max}(y))$, etc. Sincere voting may thus be viewed as "Maximax" in contrast to the "Maximin" of *prudential* voting. Cf. R. B. Braithwaite, *Theory of Games as a Tool for the Moral Philosopher* (Cambridge, Cambridge University Press, 1955).

The freedmen are thus convicted; therefore the second vote is between banishment and death:

    For banishment: acquitters and banishers;

    For death: condemners;

    Result: banishment.

He, however, proposed Procedure III. Under this procedure, with sincere voting, each group would have supported its own first preference and, since the acquitters were the most numerous single group, the result would have been acquittal.

A full account of the consequences of sincere voting under various procedures is given in the Appendices.

CHAPTER 4.

Strategies

If we are to investigate the strategic aspects of voting under such procedures, we must bring them within the scope of the theory of games.[1]

Any procedure can be represented as a game by assuming that each voter makes a plan in advance regarding the course of action he will take in every division which can arise. Any such plan may be called a "strategy"— the voter's set of strategies constitutes the complete range of such possible plans.

Formally, a strategy is simply a set of choices, one to each division.

Under Procedure Ia, for example, there are two divisions, and each voter has two choices at each. If by "1" we designate an "Aye" and by "0" a "No", the four strategies open may be identified as "00, 01, 10 and 11". One may take the motions as (i) to convict, (ii) to condemn to death, with acquittal resulting if (i) is defeated and banishment if (ii) is defeated. Then the strategies may be read:

> 00: to vote for acquittal, failing that for banishment;
>
> 01: to vote for acquittal, failing that for condemnation;

---

1. For our purposes, a game may be considered as comprising:
   i) an integer n, the number of *players*,
   ii) n finite sets S_k $1 \leq k \leq n$, of strategies,
   iii) n binary relations R_k, defined in the Cartesian product of the sets S_k.

10: to vote for conviction, and then for banishment;

11: to vote for conviction, and then for condemnation to death.

We may suppose that each voter makes his decision by selecting a strategy. Such a strategy, once chosen, provides a complete specification of his course of action at each division.[2]

Thus, if the preferences of the voters with respect to the outcomes are included, the procedure completely corresponds to a "game in normalised form".

Such a game may be given a diagrammatic representation as a "product space". Each voter may be thought of as making his choice along one axis of a three-dimensional space: by choosing a strategy he chooses a plane in that space. Specification of the strategy chosen by every voter selects a point in the space: we call such a point a *situation*.

If there are just two outcomes and three voters, we have Figure 5. The two outcomes are denoted by white and red.

The first voter's strategies are arranged diagonally, the second voter's vertically, the third voter's horizontally. This procedure is that of simple majority vote between two outcomes—thus there are three dimensions, representing the three voters, and two colours, one for each outcome. Each voter, by choosing a strategy, chooses a subset of four situations. The three choices together uniquely select one circle, the intersection of the three strategies.

2. The procedure may then be thought of as composed of:
   i) a set of strategies, one for each voter,
   ii) a partition into outcomes of the set of selections of strategies.

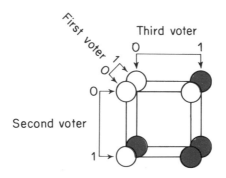

Figure 5

If we are to represent Procedure Ia in full, we must show four strategies for each voter, and thus a complete range of 64 situations. The front circle in the top left-hand corner represents that situation in which the voting is 00, 00, 00, the circle behind it that in which the voting is 01, 00, 00, and so on—the situation in which the voting is 11, 11, 11 is in the bottom right-hand corner at the back. (See Figure 6.)

In discussing procedures of type III, it is necessary to consider the cases in which no single subset receives an absolute majority of choices. We can suppose, as in the example, that one of the three groups is larger than either of the others, or, in the case of a three-voter committee, we may suppose that one of them, as chairman, has a casting as well as a deliberative vote. If we, make such an assumption, and assign the additional power to the first voter, diagonally represented, Procedure III may be portrayed as in Figure 7.

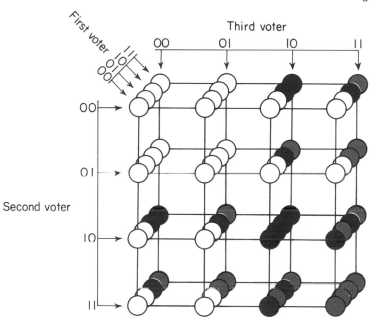

Figure 6
Procedure Ia

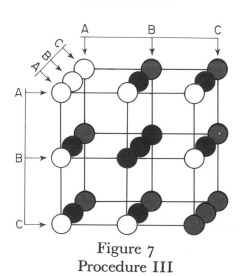

Figure 7
Procedure III

CHAPTER 5.

Individual Equilibrium

It is not always to a voter's advantage to act sincerely. In certain cases he will find that, had he chosen a different strategy, the outcome reached would have been different, and in his opinion preferable.

We may call all situations of which this is true "vulnerable". Consider the example, Procedure III, with sincere voting: the preferences are ABC, BAC, CBA, and sincere voting therefore produces the outcome A. Had the third voter voted for B at the first division, he would have obtained his second preference, B, rather than his third, A.

To say that a situation is "vulnerable" is, in a sense, to make a statement dependent on a counterfactual. "If I had voted for B, the result would have been preferable".

Formally the nature of the definition is simpler: a situation is vulnerable if another situation

    i) can be obtained from the first by substituting a strategy of at least one voter;

    ii) is preferred to it by that voter, or those voters.

Figure 8 shows how the term can be interpreted: the sincere point, at the intersection of the rows and columns, is vulnerable to the point immediately adjoining it on the left.

If a situation is "invulnerable" to all voters, we can call it an individual equilibrium. Such a situation corresponds to a "Nash equilibrium point"[1] in the theory of

1. J. Nash, "Non-cooperative Games", *Annals of Mathematics*, *54* (1951) 286-95.

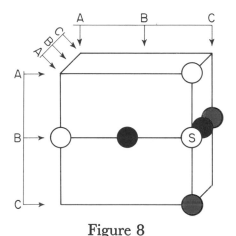

Figure 8
Procedure III
(S is a vulnerable point)

games. It is one in which each voter can say "no other strategy would have given a better outcome".

Sincere voting may or may not give an equilibrium. We have just seen how the result of sincere voting was vulnerable in the case of Procedure III; sincere voting under Procedure Ia, in that instance, would have given an equilibrium. Figure 9 exhibits this situation, showing how no preferable situation lies along any line.

The individual equilibria occurring in the case of the voting on the freedmen are indicated for the two procedures in Figures 10 and 11. The equilibria are marked "E": all other situations are vulnerable to at least one of the three voters.

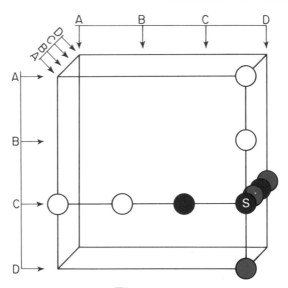

Figure 9
Procedure Ia
(S is an individual equilibrium)

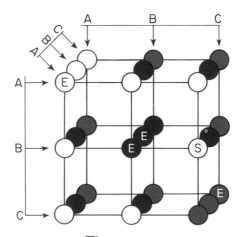

Figure 10
Procedure III
(4 Equilibria)

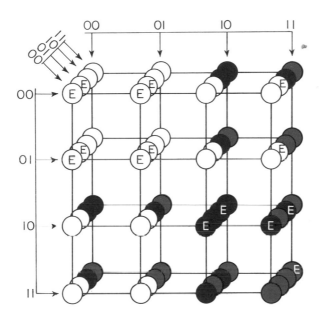

Figure 11
Procedure Ia
(15 Equilibria)

CHAPTER 6.

Admissibility

This plethora of equilibria is somewhat embarrassing: we can hardly hope to use the concept as a means of selecting particular results unless we can limit its scope somewhat more effectively.

Certain equilibria, clearly, are bogus. For example, every situation in which the voters unanimously support the same outcome is necessarily an equilibrium (by Axiom II), because no change of strategy by any single voter makes any difference to the result.

Let us attempt, therefore, to consider what possible considerations may move a voter seeking to choose a strategy. He may be totally ignorant of either the preferences or the strategies of the other voters; nevertheless, his choice is not entirely random.

Define a "contingency" as "some combination of strategies of all voters but one". Then the voter knows the result of every strategy in every contingency, but is ignorant of the contingency which will arise.

Some strategies, he can state in advance, are undesirable: for example, the condemners under Procedure Ia can definitely abandon that strategy which consists in voting for A, since it results always in an outcome either worse, or no better, than their sincere strategy.

Such a strategy, we may say, is "inadmissible".

Formally, a strategy is admissible if there is no other strategy providing

    i) in all contingencies an outcome at least as good;

    ii) in some contingency a better outcome.

Thus in every procedure each voter will have at least one admissible strategy. Sincere voting will always be admissible, but not all admissible strategies are sincere.

The admissibility test provides a means of distinguishing between equilibrium points.

In each of the cases considered in the previous chapter, there is just one admissible equilibrium: under Procedure Ia it is the sincere situation; under Procedure III it is that situation in which the acquitters vote for A, the others for B.

This uniqueness, however, cannot be relied on: in the case of Procedure Ib with the same preferences, there would have been two admissible equilibria, neither of them arising from sincere voting.

CHAPTER 7.

Straightforwardness

The only circumstances in which a voter can make his choice of strategy with absolute confidence are those in which he can be sure that, whatever contingency eventuates, his strategy will give at least as desirable an outcome as any other strategy would have done. If this is so, he may indeed fail to get what he wants, but he has the consolation that the failure was not due to any error in his choice of strategy.

We adopt the term "straightforward"[1] to describe a strategy which is thus unconditionally best. If a procedure offers a voter only one admissible strategy, then that strategy is straightforward, and conversely.

If a procedure affords a voter a straightforward strategy, we may transfer the epithet, and say that the procedure itself is straightforward for him.

A straightforward strategy is always sincere, but a sincere strategy is not necessarily straightforward.

Under what conditions will a procedure be straightforward for a voter with any given preference scale?

This question can be conclusively answered for the class of binary procedures.

We say that a scale is "weakly separated" by a division

---

1. Von Neumann and Morgenstern call such a strategy "permanently optimal"; J. McKinsey, in *Introduction to the Theory of Games* (New York, McGraw-Hill, 1952), speaks of "a strategy which non-strictly dominates all others". Since the concept is a useful one, a more manageable term for it seems desirable.

if the subsets into which the set of outcomes is divided do not overlap on the scale.

If the set of outcomes (A,B,C,D,E) is divided into the subsets (A,B,C) and (D,E) then the scale ABCDE is said to be separated by the division. A line can be drawn, cutting the scale, and such that all the members of one subset lie to the left, all the members of the other subset lie to the right.

Thus: ABC / DE

On the other hand, the division in question does not separate the scale AECDB. There is no place at which a line can be drawn so as to have (A,B,C) on one side, (D,E) on the other.

The adverb "weakly" indicates that it is permissible for one outcome to lie astride the line—the division into the subsets (A,B,C) and (C,D,E) weakly separates the scale ABCDE.

Thus: ABCDE

On the other hand, the division into (A,B,C,D) and (C,D,E) does not, since no line can be drawn fulfilling the requirements.

Formally, a division into two subsets separates a scale if the top outcome of one subset is ranked not higher than the bottom outcome of the other.[2]

Now we can assert

> THEOREM: A procedure is straightforward for a voter if and only if every division of it separates his scale.

For proof of this theorem we need to refer back to the axioms, defining a voting procedure, of Chapter 2.

---

2. For subsets x and y, if either Min (x) R_k Max (y), or Min (y) R_k Max (x).

If the voter's scale is separated by a particular division, then at that division he will be able to choose a subset whose least desirable member is as desirable as any member of the other subset. Thus he cannot regret his choice, whatever outcome is actually selected, for no other choice could have resulted in a preferable outcome.

But if even one division does not separate his scale, he will have no straightforward strategy. For then, whatever subset he chooses, there will be a possibility that its lowest-ranked member will be finally selected, whereas a higher-ranked member would have been chosen from the other subset. Therefore if his choice was decisive between the two subsets, the result is vulnerable, since he could have obtained a preferable outcome by voting differently. The same possibility exists whatever choice he makes: thus no strategy is straightforward.

It follows from this theorem that, if there are three or more outcomes, no binary procedure can be straightforward for all possible preference scales. Whatever procedure one may construct, there is always at least one scale for which it offers two or more distinct admissible strategies and therefore no straightforwardness.

We now have a means of reading off instantly, from the extensive form,

  i) whether or not the procedure is straightforward for any given preference scale;

  ii) if it is not straightforward, which of its strategies are admissible.

Thus we can say at once that Procedure Ia is straightforward for voters with scales ABC (acquitters) and CBA (condemners); it is not straightforward for voters whose scale is BAC (banishers), and offers them the two admissible strategies 01 (vote for A, vote for B) and II (vote against A, vote for B). Procedure Ia is straightforward for those voters who have A at either end of their scales, Procedure IIa for those who have A in the middle of their scales.

Procedures of type I (Ia, Ib, Ic) will therefore each be straightforward for four of the six possible strong scales by which three outcomes can be ordered. Procedures of type II (IIa, IIb, IIc) are straightforward only for two of the six.

We cannot reach such immediate conclusions for procedures of type III; it is still necessary to construct the normalised form in order to determine the straightforward strategies.

It is possible, however, to state a sufficient condition for the straightforwardness of divisional procedures.

If there is one subset which is weakly separated from every other subset, *and* if all elements of all other subsets are ranked equal, then the procedure is straightforward.

This condition is very strong, and obviously sufficient. A counter-example to its necessity is provided by the case of the chairman under Procedure III: he has a straightforward strategy, although there is no subset such that all outcomes outside it are ranked equal.

An instance of a more complete binary procedure is taken from an actual case. The circumstances have been disguised, but the structural details are unchanged.

Illustration: The Case of Jones

Jones is a candidate for employment in a library. Opinion is divided on his merits; a decision has to be reached on whether he is to be offered a senior post, a junior post, or none at all. A motion is moved by his extreme partisans:

"That Jones be appointed to the senior post". (A)

A more lukewarm section of the committee moves an amendment:

"That the word 'senior' be replaced by 'junior' ". (B)

The first vote is taken on the amendment. If it is adopted, the committee votes next on the motion as amended:

"That Jones be appointed to a junior post". (B)

This is an example of a procedure of type IIc.

The first division divides the outcomes into groups (A,C) and (B,C). Six of the twelve possible non-trivial scales fulfil the conditions slated above. Each of these scales is a fairly unlikely one: they are ACB, BCA, B(AC),[3] (AC)B, A(BC), (BC)A. Yet it is for these scales, and for them only, that the procedure is straightforward. Both his strong partisans, with scale ABC, and his opponents, scale CBA, are forced to attempt to forecast the actions of the others and each other. The same is true of those whose scales are C(AB), (AB)C, ABC, and BAC.

Let us complicate Jones' position a little by giving it further characteristics of the actual case. After a year in the junior post, his contract came up for renewal. The committee was again divided, particularly on the point whether it would be desirable to employ a qualified librarian, which Jones was not.

Some opinion favoured his promotion, but views were very divided.

After discussion, it was agreed that the following procedure should be adopted:

The motion would first be put:

1) "That a senior post be created". If passed, then,
2) "That the post be held only by a qualified librarian".

3. By B(AC) we mean that B is the voter's first preference and that A and C rank equal second.

If (2) were rejected, then there would be put:

 3) "That Mr. Jones be appointed to the senior post".

If (1) were rejected, the committee would proceed immediately to

 4) "That Mr. Jones' contract be renewed in his
  present post".

If (2) were adopted, or (3) or (4) rejected, no further vote would be taken—Jones' employment would end, and the resulting vacant post be advertised.[4]

There are five outcomes altogether:

 (A) Senior post, restricted, advertised;
 (B) Senior post, unrestricted, held by Jones;
 (C) Senior post, unrestricted, advertised;
 (D) Junior post, with Jones reappointed;
 (E) Junior post, advertised.

The division on the first motion can be shown to divide the set of outcomes into two disjunct subsets: (A,B,C) and (D,E). The whole procedure forms a tree, as shown in Figure 12.

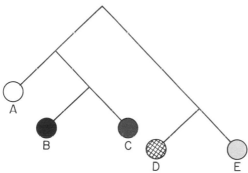

Figure 12
The Case of Jones

4. It was taken for granted that Jones would not be able to apply for the advertised post.

Three cases can be taken as representative. First, that of the voters who are strong personal supporters of Jones. Clearly, they would regard (B), his appointment to the senior post, as most desirable; also, they would rather see him continue in his junior post than not at all. Their scale is thus BD(ACE). This scale is not separated by the first division, and it is evident that these voters are in a dilemma. If they vote for the first motion, they risk affecting the creation of the senior post without securing his election to it, and thus preventing his reappointment although they could have secured it by voting differently. On the other hand, if they vote against the motion they prevent him from securing the advancement which the other voters might well have been prepared to grant him. They have no straightforward strategy, and must resort to attempting the prediction of others' behaviour. Whatever they do, they may regret.

Consider also those voters who consider Jones suitable for his present position, but who would rather see another candidate, not necessarily professionally qualified, in the senior post. If their scale is CABDE, they have no straightforward strategy, though it can never be disadvantageous for them to vote for the first motion.

Finally, consider those who favour the creation of the senior post, and feel that it should be restricted to a qualified candidate. It is immaterial whether, if this restriction cannot be achieved, they wish to retain Jones' services in either the senior or the junior capacity (or even if they would support him for one, but not for the other). In every case, they can find at least one strategy which they can adopt with a quiet mind.

Out of the 120 possible strong scales, the procedure turns out to be straightforward for only 16: the following

eight, and their converses (the converse of a scale is
obtained by simply reversing the order of preference):

ABCDE   (Straightforward strategy = 1111 "to sup-
             port every motion that reaches a vote")

ACBDE   (Straightforward strategy = 1101 "to vote
             for the creation of the senior post; if it is
             created, to support restricting it; if it is un-
             restricted, to vote against Jones' appoint-
             ment to it; but if the senior post is not
             created, to support the renewal of his
             contract")

| ABCED | DEABC | EDABC |
| ACBED | DEACB | EDACB |

CHAPTER 8.

Sophistication

If a voter does not have a straightforward strategy, it is necessary for him, to make the best use of his vote, to attempt to predict the contingency likely to arise: that is to say, how the others are likely to vote. If their strategies are not straightforward, they will face the same problem: each can make a confident choice only if he already knows the strategies to be chosen by the others: there is danger of an infinite regress.

A solution is possible, however. Let us postulate as before a committee whose members have clearly defined preference scales, and suppose that, through discussion or other means, each voter has become aware of the scales of the other voters. This does not in itself give an individual voter a secure basis for choosing his strategy, for he is still unaware of exactly what strategies his colleagues intend to choose.

However, he has one resource. Knowledge of a voter's preference is sufficient to determine his admissible strategies: thus our voter can eliminate, from the contingencies which he must consider, all those arising from the use of inadmissible strategies. This course involves, certainly, an assumption about the behaviour of the other voters, but the assumption—that only admissible strategies will be used—is at least a fairly reasonable one. For, by definition, an inadmissible strategy can in no circumstances lead to a better outcome than an admissible one would have done, and in at least one contingency it must lead to an outcome which is definitely worse.

Our voter can now consider his position. Originally, by hypothesis, he had several admissible strategies. Reducing the number of contingencies to be provided against produces a different and smaller game; in this new game, some of these strategies of his may cease to be admissible.

Formally, we may say:

A strategy is primarily admissible if there is no other strategy which produces at least as good a result in every contingency, and a better result in some contingency.

A strategy is secondarily admissible if, on the assumption that all other players use only primarily admissible strategies, it produces at least as good a result in every contingency, and a better result in some contingency.

In general, a strategy is m-arily admissible if it remains admissible on the assumption that all other players use only $(m-1)$-arily admissible strategies.

This type of argument, in effect, reaches conclusions about what *will* happen, by successively eliminating categories of events that certainly will *not* happen.[1]

---

1. This analysis was made without reference to David Gale, "A Theory of N-Person Games with Perfect Information", *Proceedings of the National Academy of Sciences, 39* (1953), 496-501, in which a somewhat similar technique is combined with a policy of equally mixing the probabilities of equivalent strategies. The essential principle involved may be traced in J. M. Keynes' *General Theory of Employment, Interest and Money:* "Professional investment may be likened to those newspaper competitions in which the competitors have to pick out the six prettiest faces from a hundred photographs, the prize being awarded to the competitor whose choice most nearly corresponds to the average preferences of the competitors as a whole; so that each competitor has to pick, not those faces

We call this type of voting "sophisticated".

In the case of the freedmen, the acquitters and the condemners have straightforward strategies under Procedure
Ia. The banishers have no straightforward strategy; however, if they assume that the other two groups will each
use straightforward strategies, then only one strategy is
ultimately admissible, that of sincere voting.

It should be emphasised that this "ultimate straightforwardness" depends on knowledge of preferences *and*
on the assumption that straightforward strategies are
always adopted. For if there was any possibility that a
majority would vote to condemn at the final division,
then it would be admissible for the banishers to vote for
acquittal at the first division.

Under Procedure III, the acquitters (being most
numerous) have a straightforward strategy. This is true
neither for the banishers nor for the condemners, each
of which have two admissible strategies. If they can
assume, however, that the acquitters will act straight-
forwardly, then for each only one strategy remains admissible: "vote for B".

Thus the "sophisticated result" corresponds to the
result which was in fact reached in the Senate. (See
figures 13, 14, 15.)

---

which he himself finds prettiest, but those which he thinks likeliest to
catch the fancy of the other competitors, all of whom are looking at the
problem from the same point of view. It is not a case of choosing those
which, to the best of one's judgement, are really the prettiest, nor even
those which average opinion genuinely thinks the prettiest. We have
reached the third degree where we devote our intelligences to anticipating
what average opinion expects the average opinion to be. And there are
some, I believe, who practice the fourth, fifth and higher degrees."

We suppose that the voters can practice the nth degree of anticipation
in this sense.

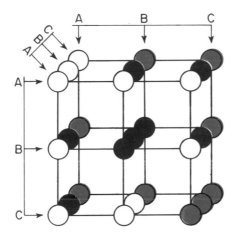

Figure 13
Procedure III
(Oth Reduction)

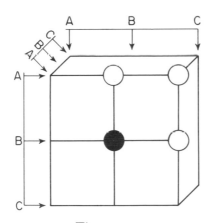

Figure 14
Procedure III
(First Reduction)

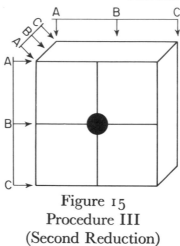

Figure 15
Procedure III
(Second Reduction)

Thus, the assumption that voting is sophisticated in this sense permits a process of successive reduction of the game space. In the cases we have considered, this reduction continues until a single point is reached that has a good title to recognition as the unique result of a kind of "hyper-rational" strategy choice by all voters.

We can prove that this completeness of reduction always occurs in binary procedures, provided that each voter's scale is strong. Call a procedure "determinate" if it reduces to a single outcome.

THEOREM: If all preferences are strong, every binary procedure is determinate.

This proof depends on the axioms of Chapter 2, from which it follows that if an outcome A is preferred to an outcome B, a strategy including a choice of B cannot be admissible. Consider the final division of a binary procedure: each voter will have just one admissible choice, and therefore only one outcome is possible. The division may thus be deleted, and this outcome substituted. The process can then be repeated for the penultimate division, and so on.

A counter-example is easily found for ternary procedures: if the scales of three voters are ABC, BCA, CBA, then the admissible strategies are

1) "vote for A";
2) "vote for B"; "vote for C";
3) "vote for C"; "vote for B".

The first reduction of the procedure, as in Figure 16, gives the subspace, which is not further reducible.

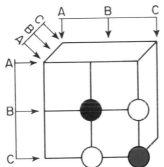

Figure 16
First Reduction:
Irreducible

This procedure appears to be determinate only in the cases in which it is primarily straightforward for all voters because their scales are of the form A(BC), etc., all outcomes but the first being of equal rank. But scales of this kind are not in general conducive to determinacy, for a voter with such indifference will have two admissible strategies at a final division between the two outcomes last on his scale. Therefore a procedure of, for example, type IV, is not determinate in such circumstances.

A procedure not within our model is that advanced by
C. L. Dodgson. Each voter writes down his scale: the
first outcome is scored 3, the second 2, the third 1. The
outcome with the greatest total of points is chosen.

We can study this procedure directly in normalised
form. Each voter has 6 strategies, corresponding to the
6 possible strong scales. Since ties may occur nevertheless,
we suppose as before that, in case of equality of score,
the choice of the first voter breaks the tie.

We discover that this procedure is straightforward for
no strong preference scale. Indeed, it offers every voter
three admissible strategies, corresponding to just those
three which may be obtained from his own scale by
reversing at most one pair of adjacent outcomes. (See
figures 17, 18, 19, 20, 21.)

We are finally left with a 2 x 2 x 2 subspace; the ultimate admissible strategies are:

1) ABC and ACB
2) BAC and CBA
3) CAB and CBA

For voter 2, sincere voting (BCA) is not ultimately
admissible.

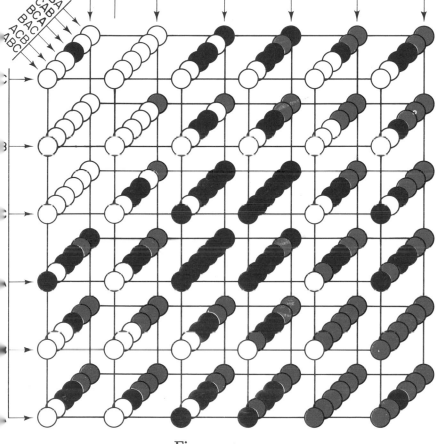

Figure 17
Procedure V

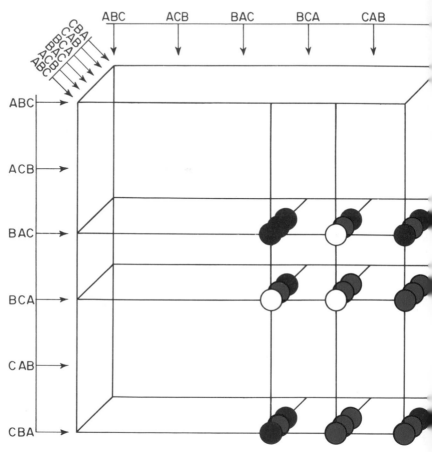

Figure 18
Procedure V
(First Reduction)

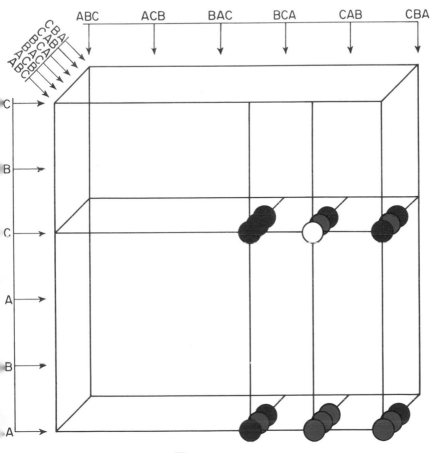

Figure 19
Procedure V
(Second Reduction)

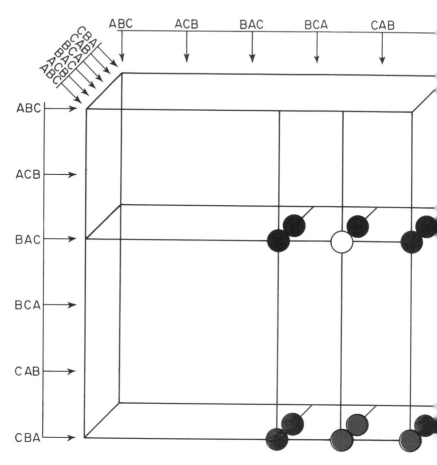

Figure 20
Procedure V
(Third Reduction)

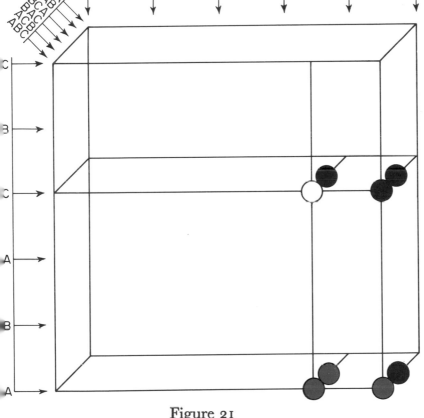

Figure 21
Procedure V
(Fourth Reduction)

CHAPTER 9.

Collective Equilibrium

Our treatment so far has concerned voters who act only as individuals, each attempting to predict the actions of others, but not cooperating explicitly with them.

Sophisticated voting assumes no cooperation; nevertheless its effects may sometimes appear to bear interpreting as implicit coalition of one group of voters against another.

Such a case is that of "The Paradox of the Chairman's Vote". Under Procedure III, we supposed that ties were broken by the designation of one of the voters as chairman, with an additional casting vote as well as his own deliberative vote. If preferences are disposed symmetrically in a three-member committee, with each outcome occurring once as first preference, once as second, and once as third, the result of sincere voting is the chairman's first choice. However, sophisticated voting has the opposite effect: precisely because the chairman's vote is worth more than that of either of the other members, the result is that his last choice is selected.

Suppose preference scales ABC (chairman), BCA, CAB. To vote for A is straightforward for the chairman; each of the other two voters has two primarily admissible strategies. However, for each of them the only secondarily admissible strategy is "vote for C". Thus the sophisticated result is C.[1]

1. This example may instructively be compared with Martin Shubik's three-person duel, in which the worst shot has the best chance of survival ("Does the fittest necessarily survive?" in *Readings in Game Theory and*

One might be tempted to say of such a case that "the chairman's strength forced the other two voters into a coalition against him". But in fact the voters have behaved entirely as isolated individuals. At most they could be said to have formed an "implicit" coalition.

Conscious and explicit cooperation between voters has not yet been provided for in our theory; this gap can be filled by extending the definition of "vulnerability".

We say that a situation is vulnerable to a set of voters if

i) there is some situation which all members of the set prefer;

ii) they can together obtain it by altering their own strategies jointly.[2]

Similarly we can generalise the definition of equilibrium and say:

A situation is an *equilibrium of order r* if it is not vulnerable to any set of r voters.[3]

Under this definition, an equilibrium of order 1 is an individual, or Nash equilibrium.

We shall show that an equilibrium of order 1 is not necessarily an equilibrium of any higher order, nor does the converse hold.

Political Behavior, New York, Doubleday, 1954). His result, however, requires extended numerical computation, while ours arises from a direct and elementary argument.

2. A situation s is an n-tuple of strategies $(s_1, s_2, \ldots s_n)$.

We call s vulnerable to a set K of voters $K \subset N$, if there is another situation $t = t_1, t_2, \ldots t_n)$ such that

i) for every K in K, $t \ P_k \ s$,

ii) for every k not in K, $s_k = t_k$.

3. See Robin Farquharson, "Sur une généralisation de la notion d'équilibrium", *C. R. Acad. Sc.*, 240 (1955), 46-48. Shubik has independently made a similar generalisation under the name of k-stability, in *Strategy and Market Structure* (New York, Wiley, 1959).

A situation which is an equilibrium of all orders, from 1 to n, we call a *collective equilibrium*.

A sophisticated result is always an individual equilibrium; it will not necessarily be a collective equilibrium.

The sense of equilibrium may be most simply expressed thus:

> There is no person or group with both the *will* and the *power* to make a change.

In the case of the freedmen, the sophisticated result is a collective equilibrium. The banishers have attained their first preference; no departure from it could command the support both of the acquitters and of the condemners. Yet neither alone has the power to make a change.

However, this will not be true in general. Let us take an example from the Senate of the United States.[4]

> A five-year $18 billion highway programme was offered by Tennessee's Democratic Senator Albert Gore . . .
>
> The Gore measure included a provision that applied to the highway programme the Davis-Bacon Act of 1931, which set up fair-pay standards for workers on federal construction projects. The Davis-Bacon Act is anathema to many Southern Democrats, who would have voted against the Gore Bill if the clause had remained. Realising this, Democrats Johnson and Gore offered to drop the Davis-Bacon proviso. If the G.O.P. leadership had been alert, the Republicans could have joined with Northern liberals in voting that the Davis-Bacon requirement stay in, then joined with the Southern-

4. *Time*, June 6, 1955, p. 15.

ers to defeat the Gore bill as a whole. They would have been acting on party principle, since the Davis-Bacon Act was a pro-labour measure originally passed under Republican auspices. But the Republicans flubbed their chance, sat silent in their chairs while Johnson and Gore got the clause out of the bill.

[In] the key vote to send the Gore bill back to committee . . . the count was 50 to 39 against recommitting the bill. Final passage of the bill did not require a roll-call vote: the Senate whooped it through and sent it to the House.

Let A = the status quo;
    B = the Gore bill with the Davis-Bacon clause;
    C = the Gore bill without the Davis-Bacon clause.

Procedure is of type IIa. Preference scales, plausibly:

Northern Democrats	BCA
Southern Democrats	CAB
Republicans	ABC

Sincere voting is primarily, but not secondarily, admissible for the Northern Democrats. The sophisticated result is C.

Yet if coalitions can form, no equilibrium exists: whatever the outcome, there exists a coalition to which it is vulnerable.

    C is vulnerable to Northerners and Republicans;
    B is vulnerable to Southerners and Republicans;
    A is vulnerable to Northerners and Southerners.

CHAPTER 10.

Information Conditions

We have so far completely neglected to discuss how far a voter may be aware of what actions have been taken by other voters.

We have tacitly assumed that, at each division, voters have been aware only of the result of previous divisions; they have been informed neither of what choices have been made at the same division by others, nor of the detailed figures of previous choices.

Yet it is evident that, when voting is public rather than by secret ballot, the choices of voters may be affected. Part of this effect may be due to actual change of preference scale in response to an authoritative example, but strategic factors are also present.

When absent voters in the French National Assembly leave proxies in the hands of their groups, these may often include such intricate instructions as

"I will vote like Mr. A, provided Mr. B. and Mr. C have voted like him; otherwise I will vote like Mr. X unless my vote risks bringing the Government down".[1]

It is evidently impossible for every voter thus to make his choices dependent on the choices of others, for not everyone can enjoy the privilege of voting last. Introduction of open voting renders asymmetrical with respect to the voters a procedure which under secret ballot permitted them all to vote simultaneously.

The assumption we have made in previous chapters

---

1. *Daily Telegraph.*

might be termed that of "minimal information". Figure
22 shows our Procedure Ia, for the case of three voters,

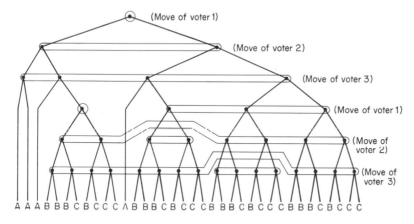

Figure 22
Procedure Ia with minimal information.
Voters know only their own choices.

represented in full as a Von Neumann game in extensive
form.[2] The red lines enclose choices in "information sets";
each voter knows the set he is in, but not his position in
that set. Figure 23 shows, for comparison, the same procedure with "perfect information". We shall refrain from
showing this procedure in normalised form: the three
voters have 8, 64, and 4096 strategies respectively.[3]

However, there is no need to draw the matrix. We can

2. Cf. Von Neumann and Morgenstern, pp. 73-78. The primitive
terms are here the set of *plays*, endpoints on the diagram; the *moves*, each
represented by a level; the "umpire's pattern of information", represented
by the tree itself; the "pattern or assignment of moves", indicated on the
right; and the "player's pattern of information", drawn in red.

3. After the elimination of redundant strategies by a "Dalkey defla-
tion". Cf. Norman Dalkey, "Equivalence of Information Patterns", in
Contributions to the Theory of Games (Princeton, Princeton University Press,
1953), 2.

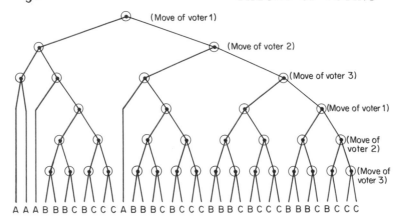

AAABBBCBCCCABBBCBCCCBBBCBCCCBBBCBCCC

Figure 23
Procedure Ia with perfect information.
Each voter knows all previous choices.

conclude at once from a theorem of Harold Kuhn[4] that there exists at least one individual equilibrium.

We cannot conclude, however, that the procedure will be straightforward, even if the preferences were such that all three voters had straightforward strategies under secret ballot.

For the first voter must now take into consideration the possibility that other voters will react to his own choices, and it is possible for them to react either positively or negatively.[5] He cannot know which; therefore no strategy can be straightforward for him.

Thus, although perfect information ensures individual equilibrium, it may actually destroy straightforwardness.

4. H. W. Kuhn, "Extensive Games and the Problem of Information", in *Contributions to the Theory of Games*, 2.

5. Positive response we may call the "bandwagon effect"; negative response, the "underdog effect". Cf. Herbert Simon, *Models of Man* (New York, Wiley, 1957).

Annexure

PLINY TO TITUS ARISTO

An extract from the *Letters* of Pliny the Younger,
translated by John, Earl of Orrery, 1752
(Yarborough Collection, Brasenose College, Vol. II, pp. 199-206)

As you are a perfect master of all acts of the legislature, both
private and public, of which last the senatorial law is a part,
I preferably choose to hear from you, whether I was guilty yes-
terday of an error in the senate, or not? I shall not attempt to
correct what is past (it is now too late) but if the like case
should again happen, I shall be glad to be instructed for the
future. . . .

A debate arose in the senate concerning the freedmen of the
consul Afranius Dexter; it being uncertain, whether he killed
himself, or whether he died by the hands of his freedmen; and
again, whether they killed him from a spirit of malice, or of
obedience. One of the senators (it is of little purpose to tell you,
I was the person) declared, that he thought these freedmen
ought to be put to the question, and afterwards released. The
sentiments of another were, that the freedmen should be banished; and of another, that they should suffer death. It was
impossible to reconcile such a diversity of opinions. What agree-
ment can be framed between the sentence for death, and the
sentence for banishment? No more indeed than between the
sentence for banishment, and for acquittal. The two latter are
however a little nearer than the two former. In both the last
cases life is spared; by the former motion it is taken away. In
the meantime, such of the senators, who had given their voice
for death, and such of them, who had declared for banishment,

57

sat together: by this temporary feint of unanimity, their dis-
union could not be discovered. I desired that the three different
opinions should be numbered; and that the two parties, who
had made a momentary truce, should be separated. I required
too, that the persons, who had voted for capital punishment,
should be entirely divided from those, who had voted for
banishment. And that both the parties, who had differently
opposed the acquittal, should not be suffered to unite together;
because it was of little consequence, that they disagreed as to
one point, while they did not agree in another. To me it
seemed an astonishing circumstance, that any person, who had
condemned the freedmen to banishment, and the slaves to
death, should be obliged to vote separately on each point; and
that the person, who had adjudged the freedmen to death, was
to be numbered among those, who had adjudged them only
to banishment. For, if the opinion of one senator ought to be
divided, because it comprehended two distinct propositions,
I did not conceive, how the opinion of any two senators could
be united, when their sentiments were so widely different. And
therefore permit me to offer to you the reasons for my decision,
in the same manner, as if I were in the senate; in the same
manner, as if the affair, which is now determined, were yet to
be adjudged. And permit me also, in my present leisure, to
connect the various thoughts, which I then expressed by starts,
amidst the interruption of noise and clamour.

Let us suppose, that three judges only had been appointed
to determine this cause; one of whom had declared, that the
freedmen ought to suffer death; another had been of opinion,
that they ought to be banished; and the third had given his
voice for their acquittal. Shall the two first opinions, because
the authors of them join together, destroy the third? Or ought
not each opinion to have as much weight as any one of the two
others? For the first bears no nearer a comparison to the second,
than the second to the third. In the senate, therefore, votes
ought to be numbered as contrary, when they are effectually
incompatible. For if one and the same person should adjudge

the criminals to be banished, and to be executed, must they,
according to that sentence, undergo banishment and death?
Or, lastly, could it be thought one single sentence, which comprehended such different decrees? When one man has determined, that they ought to die, another, that they ought to be
sent into banishment; how is it possible to affirm the determi-
nations of two persons to be only one, when, if they were pro-
nounced by any single senator, they would be deemed two
distinct awards? What is the law? Has it not expressly declared,
that the sentences for death and banishment ought to be separated? And to that purpose, is not the division of the senators
appointed in these terms? "Ye, who are of such an opinion, go
to that side: Ye, who are in every respect of a contrary opinion,
go to the side of the person, from whom you have derived your
opinion". Examine every one of these words, and consider
them well: "Ye, who are of such an opinion;" that is, ye, who
think they ought to be banished, "go to that side", that is, to
the side where sat the leader of this opinion. From whence it is
manifest, that they, who voted for death, could not remain in
the same place with those, who voted for banishment. "Ye,
who are in every respect:" You observe, that the law not content to say, "of a contrary opinion," added, "In every respect".
Can it be a doubt therefore, that they, who were for death,
thought contrary, in every respect, to those, who were for banishment? "Go to that side (of the senate-house) where the
person sits, who first made the motion, to which you adhere".
Has not the law then apparently called enforced, and driven
those, who disagree, into contrary places? Does not the consul
also, not only by the form of words, but by his hand, and ges-
ture, point out to every senator, in what part he is to stay, or
to what part he is to go? But it may be objected, that if the
votes of those, who were for death, were divided from those,
who were for banishment, the voices for an absolute acquittal
would prevail. Such an effect is not to be regarded by the persons, who give that judgement; in whom it would be indecent
to use any kind of art, or skill, that might prevent the milder

sentence from taking place. However it may be farther urged, that those, who were for death, and those, who were for banishment, should first be numbered against those, who were for acquittal, and afterwards compared among themselves; in the same manner, as at the public shews, where chance now and then sets aside and preserves some particular combatant, who afterwards contends with the conqueror of the rest: so, in the senate, we have first debates, and then again second debates; and when one opinion has prevailed, a third is ready to oppose the prevailing decision. Because, as soon as any one opinion is prevalent, the others are destroyed. For which reason it is absolutely necessary, that one and the same place should be appointed for those, who agree in sentiments, since, after sentence given, there is no such place. I will explain myself still farther: those, who are for death, ought immediately to separate themselves from those, who are for banishment, as soon as the latter have declared their opinion; or else they ought not to be permitted to separate themselves afterwards from companions, to whom they originally adhered.

But why should I assume the part of a master, when I would willingly be taught, whether these several opinions ought to have been separated or not? I obtained indeed the point, at which I aimed. I must nevertheless desire to be informed, whether I ought to have pursued my proposition, or to have receded from it, after the example of a certain person, who had given his voice for capital punishment. This senator, I know not whether convinced so much by the legality, as by the equity of the demand, desisted from his first opinion, and voted for banishment; fearing, that if the several votes were taken separately, (as according to my proposal must have been the case) those, who had voted for an entire acquittal, would have been most numerous; the numbers being much greater on that side, than on either of the other two. Upon this occasion, such persons, who had been influenced by his authority, being deferred by him, still continued to follow him, as their leader in his revolt. Thus were these three opinions reduced to two, one of which prevailed; the third, as it was overruled, had only the choice, to which of the other two it would submit.

Appendix I

Table of Results

In a committee of three members, all with strong scales, and each with a different first preference, eight combinations of scales are possible with respect to three outcomes.

For each combination, we show the result of sincere and of sophisticated voting under each of six procedures in common use.

I: The "Successive" Procedure.

Ia: The first poll is taken between A and the rest. Only if A is rejected is a second poll taken between B and C.

Ib: The first poll is taken between B and the rest. Only if B is rejected is a second poll taken between A and C.

Ic: The first poll is taken between C and the rest. Only if C is rejected is a second poll taken between A and B.

II: The "Amendment" Procedure.

IIa: The first poll is taken between B and C; the second poll is taken between A and the winner of the first poll.

IIb: The first poll is taken between A and C; the second poll is taken between B and the winner of the first poll.

IIc: The first poll is taken between A and B; the second poll is taken between C and the winner of the first poll.

III: The "Plurality" Procedure.

A single poll is taken between A, B, and C. The outcome with the greatest number of votes wins. The first voter has an additional casting vote.

IV: The "Elimination" Procedure.

The first poll is held between the pairs (A,B), (A,C) and (B,C). The pair with the greatest number of votes wins; the second poll is taken between the two members of the winning pair. The first voter has an additional casting vote.

V: The "Dodgson" Procedure.

Each voter writes down the outcomes in order of preference, without bracketing. The first outcome on his paper scores 3 points, the second 2 points, and the third 1 point. The outcome with the greatest total of points is chosen. The first voter has a casting vote in addition.

VI: The "Alternative Vote" Procedure.

Each voter writes down the outcomes in order of preference, without bracketing. The outcome listed first on his paper scores 1; the outcome with the smallest total score is eliminated. The papers are then reexamined, and the outcome now ranking first on the greatest number of papers is chosen. The first voter has a casting vote only.

CONCLUSIONS

If voting is sincere, the later a proposal is voted on, the better its chance.

Procedure Ia, which puts A first, is disadvantageous to A.

Procedure IIa, which puts A last, is advantageous to A.

If voting is sophisticated, the earlier a proposal is voted on, the better its chance.

Procedure Ia is advantageous to A.

Procedure IIa is disadvantageous to A.

Therefore: to favour a proposal, put it last if the voters are sincere, but if they are sophisticated, put it first.

If voting is sincere, a voter with both a deliberative and a casting vote gets his way more often than a voter with only a deliberative vote. A voter with only a casting vote gets his way less often than a voter with a deliberative vote.

If voting is sophisticated, a voter with both a deliberative and a casting vote gets his way *less* often than a voter with only a deliberative vote. A voter with only a casting vote gets his way *more* often than a voter with a deliberative vote.

Therefore, to get your way, seek extra power in a sincere committee, but shun extra power in a sophisticated committee.

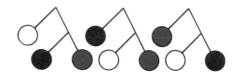

	I a	Ib	Ic
ABC, BAC, CAB			
sincere	B	A	A
sophisticated	A	A	A
ABC, BAC, CBA			
sincere	B	A	B
sophisticated	B	B	B
ABC, BCA, CAB*			
sincere	B	C	A
sophisticated	A	B	C
ABC, BCA, CBA			
sincere	B	C	B
sophisticated	B	B	B
ABC, BAC, CAB			
sincere	C	A	A
sophisticated	A	A	A
ABC, BAC, CBA*			
sincere	C	A	B
sophisticated	A	B	C
ABC, BCA, CAB			
sincere	C	C	A
sophisticated	C	C	C
ABC, BCA, CBA			
sincere	C	C	B
sophisticated	C	C	C

* = "cyclic" preferences.

	IIa	IIb	IIc
ABC, BAC, CAB			
sincere	A	A	A
sophisticated	A	A	A
ABC, BAC, CBA			
sincere	B	B	B
sophisticated	B	B	B
ABC, BCA, CAB*			
sincere	A	B	C
sophisticated	C	A	B
ABC, BCA, CBA			
sincere	B	B	B
sophisticated	B	B	B
ABC, BAC, CAB			
sincere	A	A	A
sophisticated	A	A	A
ACB, BAC, CBA*			
sincere	A	B	C
sophisticated	B	C	A
ACB, BCA, CAB			
sincere	C	C	C
sophisticated	C	C	C
ACB, BCA, CBA			
sincere	C	C	C
sophisticated	C	C	C

* = "cyclic" preferences.

	III	IV
ABC, BAC, CAB		
sincere	A	A
sophisticated	A	A
ABC, BAC, CBA		
sincere	A	B
sophisticated	B	B
ABC, BCA, CAB*		
sincere	A	A
sophisticated	C	C
ABC, BCA, CBA		
sincere	A	B
sophisticated	A, B, C	B
ACB, BAC, CAB		
sincere	A	A
sophisticated	A	A
ACB, BAC, CBA*		
sincere	A	A
sophisticated	B	B
ACB, BCA, CAB		
sincere	A	C
sophisticated	C	A, C
ACB, BCA, CBA		
sincere	A	C
sophisticated	A, B, C	B, C

* = "cyclic" preferences.

	V	VI
ABC, BAC, CAB		
sincere	A	B
sophisticated	A	A
ABC, BAC, CBA		
sincere	B	B
sophisticated	B	B
ABC, BCA, CAB*		
sincere	A	B
sophisticated	C	A
ABC, BCA, CBA		
sincere	B	B
sophisticated	A,B,C,	B
ACB, BAC, CAB		
sincere	A	C
sophisticated	A	A
ABC, BAC, CBA*		
sincere	A	C
sophisticated	B	A
ABC, BCA, CAB		
sincere	C	C
sophisticated	C	C
ACB, BCA, CBA		
sincere	C	C
sophisticated	A, B, C	C

* = "cyclic" preferences.

Appendix II

The Game-Theoretical Framework

> All things began in order, so shall
> they end, and so begin again; according
> to the ordainer of order and mystical
> mathematics of the city of heaven.
>
> SIR THOMAS BROWNE

The *Theory of Games and Economic Behavior* is a mathematical theory of rational action. It is intended by its authors to provide "an exact description of the endeavor of the individual to obtain a maximum of utility or . . . the entrepreneur a maximum of profit" in terms both more rigorous and more general than those hitherto current in economic and social theory.

The "utility" whose pursuit constitutes the game is required to possess a fully numerical character. Not only is it cardinally measurable, but it is completely transferable between players, and continuously divisible. Its properties are thus more those of "profit" than of "utility" in its sense of individual satisfaction.

> Satisfactions cannot be added. Therefore it is meaningless to speak of the happiness of the community as the sum total of the happiness of individuals, and the happiness of an individual as the sum total of his satisfactions . . .
>
> One can say when one has more or less satisfaction, but one cannot say how much one has.[1]

---

1. I. M. D. Little, *A Critique of Welfare Economics* (Oxford, Oxford University Press, 1950).

Not all the cardinal properties of "payoffs" enter into the analysis of "two-person zero-sum games". If the interests of two players are directly opposed, the question of transfers between them does not arise. It is sufficient that each player should possess a private utility index, by which he is enabled to compare not only payoffs themselves, but also "prospects" consisting of joint probability distributions of payoffs. To this end it is sufficient that ratios of differences between payoffs should be stipulated; nothing need be known or postulated regarding the ratios of payoffs themselves, either for one player or between the two players. Only the ghost of cardinality remains.

For the theory of "n-person games", or even of two-person games which are not zero-sum, a ghost does not suffice. Fully numerical cardinality must be resurrected. Individual utility is comparable between players, transferable and divisible: the game is invariant under linear transformation of the payoffs only if the same transformation is applied to the payoff schedule of every player.

It does not seem accidental that the theory of "n-person games" has been found less satisfactory than that of two-person zero-sum games. For if utility is unrestrictedly transferable and divisible, instability indefinitely propagates itself. Any increment of utility, however small, is sufficient to affect any number of players, however large.

But the concepts of imputation and dominance[2] lead to no satisfactory notion of "solution" for n-person games, since in general *every* imputation is dominated by some other imputation.

---

2. An imputation is a schedule prescribing the share of each player in the proceeds of the game. An imputation is said to dominate another imputation if some set of players exists such that
  i) they can together be sure of obtaining as much as the dominating imputation allots them;
  ii) each of them receives more according to the dominating than according to the dominated imputation.

This conclusion banishes all hope of attaining a "determinate" theoretical result for games in which coalitions play a part. The sense of "solution" adopted[3] is extremely weak, and has been found of comparatively little relevance to problems of group decision.

It seems to have been dissatisfaction with this state of affairs which impelled J. F. Nash, Jr., to develop his analysis of "noncooperative games". Discarding altogether the apparatus of coalitions and "characteristic functions" on which the old theory rested, he treats each individual as unable to communicate or collaborate with the others. Thus utility recovers the status it held in the two-person zero-sum game: it is personal to each player, and no comparison between the utility or different individuals need be made.

His point of view is thus well adapted to the game representation of politics insofar as it treats of a world in which there are no bribes or share-outs.

However, the absence of communication between players means that no account can be taken of a most central aspect of political life—the formation of parties, caucuses, and blocs.

We propose, therefore, an approach which is distinct both from that of Von Neumann and from that of Nash, in which aspects of both their treatments can be reconciled.

The theory of Von Neumann, then, prescribes both side-payments[4] and coalitions; that of Nash permits neither. We shall advocate the use of a theory including coalitions, but with side-payments excluded.

This limitation has three advantages.

3. In which a solution is conceived not as a single imputation but as a set of imputations such that
   i) no imputation in the solution is dominated by an imputation also in the solution;
   ii) every imputation outside the solution is dominated by some imputation in the solution.
4. The term "side-payments" is used to designate transfers of utility between players.

First, by excluding direct money payments outside the game, it conforms not only to the ethics of most card games and some markets, but also to the spirit of the Corrupt and Illegal Practices Prevention Act, 1883.

Secondly, it permits an escape from the multiplicity and the nonuniqueness of "solutions" in Von Neumann's sense—a situation can now exist in which domination becomes asymmetrical and transitive.

Thirdly, it permits the whole theory to be expressed in ordinal terms.

An ordinal reformulation of game theory could take several forms. One of these would be an expansion of the usual representation by including as explicit pure strategies all possible probability distributions and all possible schedules of side-payments, and then employ a utility function mapping each n-tuple of such strategies (of which there would be an infinite number) onto an ordered set. It would then be possible to define all the concepts of the theory in terms appropriate to the new representation.

Such a formulation would require notational changes, but nothing more. Each of its concepts would correspond exactly to a concept of the usual theory, and the new theory would operationally be completely equivalent to the old. A restatement on these lines has been sketched by Lloyd Shapley and Martin Shubik.[5]

We propose a more radical course. Ordinal preferences are to be treated as fundamental, and all the concepts of the theory defined directly in their terms. No use can be made even of ratios of differences; therefore utilities cannot be combined with probabilities, still less compared or transferred.

By adopting this course, we commit ourselves to an austerity which should satisfy even the most conceptually parsimonious of welfare economists. Our results will therefore be more re-

5. "Solution of N-Person Games with Ordinal Utilities", *Econometrica*, *21* (1953), 348 (abstract).

stricted in method, and correspondingly more general in scope.
Though our diet is Spartan, anything we can prepare from our
scanty larder will be digestible not only by our fellow ascetics,
but also by those accustomed to the richer fare of Cardinal
Club dinners with Sir Dennis Robertson.[6]

The ordinal theory which emerges proves to lack many of
the familiar features of the original theory, but also to possess
some compensating advantages.

No result expressed in terms of pure strategies is affected;
the "perfect information theorem", and its extension by Kuhn,
stand unchanged.

The "strict determinacy" of two-person zero-sum games is
sacrificed. Since strategies cannot be mixed, there can exist
games without saddle-points: similarly, not every n-person
game need possess a Nash equilibrium.

On the other hand, n-person game theory seems to be in a
more satisfactory condition. It is no longer the case that the possibility of coalitions prevents any determinate solution. There
can exist situations that are not dominated by any others.[7]

Finally, the gulf between two-person zero-sum games and
games in general disappears. All concepts can now readily be
developed, and all definitions expressed, in n-person terms
from the outset. Thus this approach is in conformity with the
counsels of Von Neumann and Morgenstern's final chapter, in
which they ponder the consequences of their utility assumptions, and conjecture that

> A unified treatment for the entire theory of the n-person
> game—without the (as it now appears) artificial halt at
> the zero-sum two-person game and the characteristic func-
> tion—may therefore *in fine* prove to be the remedy for these
> difficulties.

---

6. "Utility and All What?" *Economic Journal*, *64*, (1954), 669.

7. Cf. Von Neumann and Morgenstern, p. 603. If utility is transferable
and indefinitely divisible, any gain, however small, can be divided so as
to give a positive benefit to every member of any coalition, however large.

The content of our ordinal model can be set out in perceptibly simpler terms than that of the cardinal theory. We require only a set of voters, each with a set of strategies and a connected and transitive preference ordering in the set of selections of strategies.

We define a "game" (in normalised form) as a triple

$$(n, S_k, R_k)$$

where   n is an integer;

      S_k, defined for $1 \leq k \leq n$, is a finite set;

      R_k, defined for $1 \leq k \leq n$, is a binary relation in the set product S,

$$S = \prod_{k=1}^{n} S_k$$

Each integer k, $1 \leq k \leq n$, we call a "player"; each element of the set $S_k = (s_k, t_k, \ldots)$ we call a "strategy"; each element of the set $S = (s, t, u, \ldots)$ we call a "situation"; each element q_k of the quotient set $Q_k - S/S_k$ we call a "contingency".

We assume, for any three situations s, t, u (not necessarily distinct) in S:

  i) either $s\ R_k\ t$ or $t\ R_k\ s$ or both;

  ii) if $s\ R_k\ t$ and $t\ R_k\ u$, then $s\ R_k\ u$.

If $s\ R_k\ t$ and not $t\ R_k\ s$, we write $s\ P_k\ t$; if both $s\ R_k\ t$ and $t\ R_k\ s$, we write $s\ I_k\ t$. If for all players, $k\ s\ I_k\ t$, we write $s\ I_N\ t$.

The relation P_k is irreflexive, asymmetrical, and transitive: the relations I_k and I_N are reflexive, symmetrical, and transitive.

By N we designate the set of n players.

The relation I_N partitions S into equivalence classes. Each element m of the set $M = S/I_N$ we call an "outcome".

A situation $s = (s_1, s_2, \ldots s_n)$ is called "vulnerable" to a set

---

The abandonment of this assumption results not only in increased applicability to certain realities (since one handful of silver will not stretch to buy the defection of indefinitely many politicians) but also a more satisfactory and definite theoretical result.

K of players, $K \subset N$, if there is a situation $t = (t_1, t_2, \ldots t_n)$ such that

    i) if $k \in K$, then $t\ P_k\ s$;

    ii) if $k \notin K$, then $t_k = s_k$.

A situation is called an "equilibrium of order r" if it is not vulnerable to any set of exactly r players. A situation is called a "strong equilibrium" if it is not vulnerable to any set of players.

A game is called a "Pareto game" if, whenever for a player k and two situations s, t, in S, $s\ P_k\ t$, then for some other player j, $t\ P_j\ s$.

An equilibrium of order 1 is not necessarily an equilibrium of any higher order, nor is an equilibrium of order r necessarily an equilibrium of any other order, higher or lower. Every situation of a Pareto game is an equilibrium of order n; it follows that in a two-person Pareto game, every equilibrium of order 1 is also a strong equilibrium.

All the strong equilibria of a two-person Pareto game are in the same outcome.

Suppose s, t to be strong equilibria, $s = (s_1, s_2)$, $t = (t_1, t_2)$. Consider the situations $u = (s_1, t_2)$ and $v = (t_1, s_2)$. By the definition of equilibrium, $s\ R_1\ v$, $t\ R_1\ u$; $s\ R_2\ u$, $t\ R_2\ v$. Since the game is a Pareto game, $v\ R_2\ s$, $u\ R_2\ t$; $u\ R_1\ s$, $v\ R_1\ t$. By transitivity, $s\ R_1\ t$, $t\ R_1\ s$; $s\ R_1\ t$, $t\ R_1\ s$. By definition, $s\ I_1\ t$ and $S\ I_2\ t$. Therefore we can conclude that $s\ I_N\ t$.

A strategy s_k is called "admissible" if there is no other strategy t_k such that

    i) for every q_k, $(t_k, q_k)\ R_k\ (s_k, q_k)$, and

    ii) for some q_k, $(t_k, q_k)\ P_k\ (s_k, q_k)$.

The set S_k must contain at least one admissible strategy. We call the set of its admissible strategies its first reduction $\text{Red}^1 S_k$.

$\text{Red}^1 S$, the first reduction of S, is defined as $\prod_{k=1}^{n} \text{Red}^1 S_k$.

$\text{Red}^1 S_k$ thus $= \text{Red}^1 S / \text{Red}^1 Q_k$. $\text{Red}^0 S = S$, $\text{Red}^2 S = \text{Red}^1 \text{Red}^1 S$, and so on.

In general, we call a strategy s_k "m-arily admissible" if for all strategies t_k in $Red^{m-1}S_k$

i) for every q_k in $Red^{m-1}Q_k$, (s_k,q_k) R_k (t_k,q_k), or

ii) for some q_k in $Red^{m-1}Q_k$, (s_k, q_k) P_k (t_k,q_k).

A strategy s_k that is m-arily admissible for all values of m is called "ultimately" admissible. The set of all ultimately admissible strategies forms the ultimate reduction of S, Red^uS.

If for every s and t in Red^uS, s I_N t, every point of Red^uS falls within the same outcome, and we call the game "determinate."

If a game is determinate, every situation of its ultimate reduction is an equilibrium of order 1 in the original game. Our final diagram shows such a situation.

FINAL DIAGRAM

Once there was a club run by a Miser, a Prohibitionist, and an Alcoholic. The Prohibitionist proposed a clubhouse; the Alcoholic was in favour, provided it had a bar. The Miser was against the clubhouse, and even more strongly against equipping it with a bar. There could be no bar without a clubhouse: thus the outcomes were

A) the absence of a clubhouse,

B) a barless clubhouse,

C) a clubhouse with a bar.

Their scales, of course, were:

Miser, ABC,

Prohibitionist BAC,

Alcoholic, CAB.

They used Procedure I: a first poll between A and the rest; only if A was defeated, a second poll between B and C.

The sincere result would have had the outcome B: a barless clubhouse, a situation vulnerable to the Alcoholic. But they were all sophisticated, and thus though only the Miser had a straightforward strategy, the procedure was determinate. It

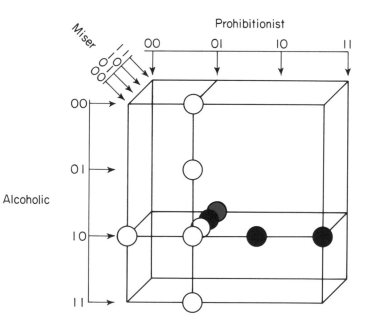

Appendix III

A Game as "Model" for
Du Contrat Social

Rules:
1) There are five ordinary players, and a Bank.
2) At each round the players are divided into two teams, Team Three of three players and Team Two of two players. Membership of the teams rotates, so that in ten rounds each player is in Team Three six times and in Team Two four times.
3) At each round every player may nominate one or other of the two teams.
4) The Banker then chooses any nominated team, and pays each of its members £10, collecting £10 from each member of the other team.

THE "STATE OF NATURE"

If each player always nominates his own team, and the Banker always chooses Team Two, then in ten rounds every player will win four times and lose six times—net loss £20. No player can improve his position by changing his behaviour.

In this game, then, each player has a straightforward strategy; but if all players follow their straightforward strategies, they all lose in the long run.

"Je suppose les hommes parvenus à ce point où les obstacles qui nuisent à leur conservation dans l'état de nature l'emportent par leur résistance, sur les forces que chaque individu peut employer pour se maintenir dans cet état. Alors, cet état primitif ne peut plus subsister; et le genre humain périrait s'il ne changeait sa manière d'être."[1]

1. J. J. Rousseau, *Du Contrat Social*.

THE "SOCIAL CONTRACT"

If all five players agree to form an Assembly, and to nominate only the team selected by a majority vote, they can together improve their position very much. The Banker's hands are then tied—if each player always votes for his own team in the Assembly, and abides by the verdict, then only Team Three will be nominated, and the Banker will be obliged to choose it. In ten rounds every player will win six times and lose four times—net gain £20. No player can improve his position by voting against his team in the Assembly—in fact, he will definitely make it worse. On the other hand, a player can gain a temporary advantage by departing from the verdict of the Assembly in the subsequent game, and nominating his own team when he is in Team Two.

" 'Trouver une forme d'association qui défend et protège de toute la force commune la personne et les biens de chaque associé, et par laquelle, s'unissant à tous, n'obéisse qu'à lui-même, et reste aussi libre qu'auparavant'. Tel est le problème fondamental dont le Contrat Social donne la solution."

"Tous, étant nés égaux et libres, n'aliènent leur liberté que pour leur utilité."

"Si l'opposition des intérêts particuliers a rendu nécessaire l'établissement des sociétés, c'est l'accord de ces mêmes intérêts qui l'a rendu possible. C'est ce qu'il y a de commun dans ces différents intérêts qui forme le lien social; et s'il n'y avait pas quelque point dans lequel tous les intérêts s'accordent, nulle société ne saurait exister."

"Il y a souvent bien de la différence entre la volonté de tous et la volonté générale; celle-ci ne regarde qu'à l'intérêt commun; l'autre regarde â l'intérêt privé, et ce n'est qu'une somme de volontés particulières; mais ôte de ces mêmes volontés les plus et les moins qui s'entredétruisent, reste pour somme des différences la volonté générale."

"Afin donc que le pacte social ne soit pas en vain formulaire, il renforme tacitement cet engagement, qui seul peut donner la force aux autres, que quiconque refusera d'obérir à la volonté générale y sera contraint par tout le corps: ce qui ne signifie autre chose sinon qu'on le forcera d'être libre."

THE "PARTY SYSTEM"

If three players combine to form a Party, and agree to vote in the Assembly not each for his own team, but all three for the team which contains the greater number of Party members, they can improve their position still further. In this case, whenever Team Two contains two Party members, it will be chosen by the Assembly, and therefore all players will be obliged to nominate it. In ten rounds, each Party member will win seven times and lose only three times—net gain £40. The Party members now are each £20, together £60, better off than under the Social Contract. The two other players, however, each win only three times and lose seven times—net loss £40. Thus together they are £120 worse off than under the Social Contract, and £40 worse off than under the State of Nature.

"Si, quand le peuple sufisamment informé délibère, les citoyens n'avaient aucune communication entre eux, du grand nombre des petites différences résulterait toujours la volonté générale, et la déliberation serait toujours bonne. Mais quand il se fait des brigues, des associations partielles aux dépens de la grande, la volonté de chacune des ces associations devient générale par rapport à ses membres, et particulière par rapport à l'Etat: on peut dire alors qu'il n'a plus autant de votants que d'hommes, mais seulement autant que d'associations."

"Il importe donc, pour avoir bien l'énoncé de la volunté générale, qu'il n'y ait pas de societé partielle dans l'État, et que chaque citoyen n'opine que d'après lui; ... ces précautions sont les seules bonnes pour que la volonté générale soit toujours éclairée, et que le peuple ne se trompe point."

In the State of Nature, each player has a straightforward strategy—the unique admissible equilibrium leads to a mean loss of £20 per player every ten rounds.

The formation of an Assembly improves the position of each

player: however, it is necessary that its decisions should be enforceable, since certain players are required to follow inadmissible strategies. Ability to make such a contract is, nevertheless, unquestionably to the players' advantage.

Once the Assembly is in effect, sincere voting in it is the only admissible strategy for each player. Such voting constitutes an equilibrium of order 1, 2, 4, and 5, but not of order 3, since a coalition of exactly three players can improve the position of all its members by concerted departure from sincerity. And, being committed to the contract, the excluded players have no defence. Thus we secure a rationale by which to explain Rousseau's hostility to the existence of political parties, and a means of interpreting his assertions which permits many of his apparent inconsistencies to be reconciled.

Bibliography

Arrow, K. J., *Social Choice and Individual Values*, Cowles Commission Monograph 12, New York, Wiley, 1951.

Beale, Martin, and Michael Drazin, "Sur une note de Farquharson", *C. R. Acad. Sc.*, *245* (1956), 123.

Berge, Claude, *Sur une théorie ensembliste des jeux alternatifs*, (doctoral thesis), Paris, Gauthier-Villars, 1953.

Birch, B. J., "On Games with Almost Complete Information", *Proceedings of the Cambridge Mathematical Society*, *51* (1955), 275-87.

Black, Duncan, "On the Rationale of Group Decision Making", *Journal of Political Economy*, *56* (1948), 23-24.

———, "The Decisions of a Committee Using a Special Majority", *Econometrica*, *16* (1948), 246-61.

———, and R. A. Newing, *Committee Decisions with Complementary Valuation*, London, Hodge, 1951.

Blackwell, David, and M. A. Girshick, *Theory of Games and Statistical Decisions*, New York, Wiley, 1954.

Braithwaite, R. B., *Scientific Explanation*, Cambridge, Cambridge University Press, 1953.

———, *Theory of Games as a Tool for the Moral Philosopher*, Cambridge, Cambridge University Press, 1955.

Brown, G. W., "Iterative Solutions of Games by Fictitious Play", in T. Koopmans, *Activity Analysis of Production and Allocation* (New York, Wiley, 1951), pp. 374-76.

Bourbaki, N., *Théorie des ensembles*, Livre I, Chapitre II, Paris, Hermann, 1954.

Coulson, C. A., *The Spirit of Applied Mathematics*, Oxford, Clarendon Press, 1953.

Dalkey, Norman, "Equivalence of Information Patterns and Essentially Determinate Games", in *Contributions to the Theory of Games, 2*, Princeton, N.J., Princeton University Press, 1953.

Farquharson, Robin, "Sur une généralisation de la notion d'équilibrium", *C. R. Acad. Sc., 240* (1955), 46-48.

—— "Straightforwardness in Voting Procedures", *Oxford Economic Papers, 8* (1956), 80-89.

—— "Strategic Information in Games and in Voting", in *Information Theory*, ed. Colin Cherry, London, Butterworths, 1956.

Gale, David, "A Theory of N-Person Games with Perfect Information", *Proc. Nat. Acad. Sc., U.S.A., 39* (1953), 496-501.

——, H. W. Kuhn, and A. W. Tucker, "Reduction of Game Matrices", in *Contributions to the Theory of Games, 2*, Princeton, N. J., Princeton University Press, 1953.

Guilbaud, G. T., "Lecons sur les éléments principaux de la théorie mathématique des jeux", in *Stratégies et décisions economiques*, Paris, Centre National de la Recherche Scientifique, 1954.

Hicks, J. R. *A Revision of Demand Theory*, Oxford, Clarendon Press, 1956.

Hurwicz, Leonid, "What Has Happened to the Theory of Games?" *American Economic Review, 65* (1953), 398-405.

Kuhn, H. W. "Extensive Games and the Problem of Information" in *Contributions to the Theory of Games, 2*, Princeton, N. J., Princeton University Press, 1953.

Little, I. M. D., *A Critique of Welfare Economics*, Oxford, Oxford University Press, 1950.

Luce, R. Duncan, and Howard Raiffa, *Games and Decisions*, New York, Wiley, 1957.

May, K. O., "A Set of Independent Necessary and Sufficient Conditions for Simple Majority Decision", *Econometrica, 20* (1952), 680-84.

————, "A Note on the Complete Independence of the Conditions for Simple Majority Decision", *Econometrica*, *21* (1952), 680-84.

McKinsey, J. C. C. *Introduction to the Theory of Games*, New York, McGraw-Hill, 1952.

Nash, J. F., "Non-cooperative Games", *Annals of Mathematics*, *54* (1951), 286-95.

Prior, Arthur, *Formal Logic*, Oxford, Clarendon Press, 1955.

Russell, Bertrand, *The Principles of Mathematics*, London, Allen and Unwin, 1903.

Shapley, Lloyd, and Martin Shubik, "Solution of N-Person Games with Ordinal Utilities", *Econometrica*, *21* (1953), 348 (abstract).

Shubik, Martin, *Readings in Game Theory and Political Behavior*, New York, Doubleday, 1954.

————, *Strategy and Market Structure*, New York, Wiley, 1959.

Simon, Herbert, *Models of Man, Social and Rational*, New York, Wiley, 1957.

Vajda, S., *Theory of Games and Linear Programming*, London, Methuen, 1956.

Von Neumann, John, and Oskar Morgenstern, *Theory of Games and Economic Behavior*, 3d ed. Princeton, N.J., Princeton University Press, 1953.

Wald, Abraham, *Statistical Decision Functions*, New York, Wiley, 1950.

Williams, J. D., *The Compleat Strategyst, Being a Primer on Theory of Games*, New York, McGraw-Hill, 1954.